Read & Respo

Ages 5~7

PAGE 1

Read & Respond

Ages
5~7

Author: Jean Evans

Commissioning Editor: Rachel Mackinnon

Editor: Tracy Kewley

Assistant Editor: Sarah Sodhi

Series Designer: Anna Oliwa

Designer: Liz Gilbert

Cover Image: Nicola Bayley

Illustrations: Nicola Bayley and Cathy Hughes

Text © 2010 Jean Evans © 2010 Scholastic Ltd

Designed using Adobe InDesign

Published by Scholastic Ltd, Book End,
Range Road, Witney,
Oxfordshire OX29 0YD
www.scholastic.co.uk

Printed by Bell & Bain
1 2 3 4 5 6 7 8 9   0 1 2 3 4 5 6 7 8 9

British Library Cataloguing-in-Publication Data
A catalogue record for this book is available from the British Library.
ISBN 978-1407-11894-9

Acknowledgements
The publishers gratefully acknowledge permission to reproduce
the following copyright material: **Walker Books** for use of extracts,
illustrations and the cover from *The Mousehole Cat* by Antonia
Barber and illustrated by Nicola Bayley. Text © 1990 Antonia
Barber; Illustrations © 1990 Nicola Bayley. (1990, Walker Books).
Every effort has been made to trace copyright holders for the works
reproduced in this book, and the publishers apologise for any
inadvertent omissions.

The Mousehole Cat

About the book

The Mousehole Cat retells the dramatic and moving tale of the Cornish legend of Tom Bawcock who saved the people of Mousehole by going fishing in a huge storm. In this version of the tale, Tom is accompanied by his brave cat Mowzer, who tames the Great Storm-Cat with the sweetness of her singing so that the little fishing boat can sail out of the harbour and Tom can catch fish to bring back to the hungry villagers. The story ends happily with a huge feast to celebrate the return of the heroes and the end of hunger. Wonderful artwork by Nicola Bayley, from exquisite full-page illustrations to intricately detailed friezes and borders, and rich and imaginative language from Antonia Barber, ensures an entrancing experience to all who read it.

The Mousehole Cat is an example of a familiar legend embellished by the author's imaginative description of the characters, setting and events and the illustrator's visual perception of these descriptions. It will inspire children to take ordinary events from their own lives and familiar stories passed on by their families, and extend and develop them into new stories. The importance of considering the needs of others is emphasised as Tom and Mowzer put all thoughts of personal danger behind them to save their friends. Children's understanding of the main characters, particularly their strength of determination in overcoming the Great Storm-Cat, can be developed through drama and role play. As the children take part, their own appreciation of differences between reality and fantasy will be enhanced and they will sympathise with Tom and Mowzer's dilemma and desire to help their friends. Reading about their unhesitating actions will raise children's awareness of the importance of supporting family and friends. The book will also help to develop children's values and encourage them to feel a sense of belonging within their own community.

Shared reading of the text provides excellent opportunities for teaching and applying Key Stage 1 word level skills, and to develop children's understanding of sentence construction and punctuation. The book can be used to motivate children into using their imaginations to compose exciting stories and invent strong characters.

About the author

Antonia Barber is an award-winning author who has written a number of books for children, including *Catkin*, *The Ghosts*, *The Frog Bride* and the *Dancing Shoes* series. She lives in Kent but has a harbourside cottage in Mousehole, the setting that inspired *The Mousehole Cat*.

About the illustrator

Nicola Bayley is best known for her detailed illustrations of cats. She has illustrated a wide range of children's books and was shortlisted for the Kate Greenaway Medal for *Katje the Windmill Cat*. Nicola lives in London.

Facts and figures

The Mousehole Cat was the winner of the British Book Award for the Illustrated Children's Book of the Year and the British Design Production Award (Children's Books). It was also shortlisted for the Smarties Prize, the Kate Greenaway Medal and the Children's Book Award.

Guided reading

Introducing the book

Show the children the book before starting to read so that they can focus on the title and cover, and make predictions about the story. Begin by exploring the illustration on the front cover together. Look at the image of the man and his cat in the box and ask the children to describe them. Ask: *Do you think the man or the cat is the main character? Can you tell whether the man is old or young, and the type of work he does, by his appearance? What can you say about the cat? Do you think the cat belongs to the man in the picture?* Encourage the children to consider people they know, past experiences or stories they have read to inform their responses. Now look at the illustration surrounding this box and on the back cover. Ask: *Can we tell where the story might be set from these illustrations? Perhaps it is set near the sea, or on a boat. Can you tell what type of boat it is?*

Read the title and ask: *Who is the Mousehole Cat? Might she be the cat on the cover? Why do you think she is called a 'mousehole' cat?* Draw attention to the names Antonia Barber and Nicola Bayley and establish who is the author and who is the illustrator of the book. (You can find out more about them on the first page of the book to extend this discussion.) Encourage the children to name the authors and illustrators of some of their favourite books and discuss the work of an illustrator.

Turn to the back cover and read the short paragraph that introduces the story. Say: *There are two cats mentioned, Mowzer and the Great Storm-Cat. Do you think one of them is the cat on the front cover? Can you guess who the man on the cover might be?* Discuss the meaning of *dramatic and moving Cornish tale*.

Initial reading

Plan to make your initial reading of *The Mousehole Cat* an enjoyable experience. Read clearly and expressively, encouraging participation, for example, by asking the children to build up mood and atmosphere by joining in with vocal effects to mimic the sounds made by Mowzer and the Great Storm-Cat. Indicate words by moving along them with a finger or pointer as you read, and remember to pause at significant points to ask the children what they think will happen next or to predict a word or phrase. For example: *Do you think Mowzer will stay in her warm armchair by the range, or follow Tom out into the great storm? What do you think might happen to Tom and Mowzer as they sail into the storm?*

As you continue to read, ensure that children understand the text through appropriate comments and queries. For example: *Tom says they will be saved if they bring this haul home. What do you think a 'haul' is?* If necessary, set up a practical activity to support understanding, in this case 'netting a haul' of plastic fish with a small fishing net and filling a bucket.

Encourage the children to consider how characters are feeling as the story progresses by asking them how they would feel in a similar situation. Ask: *Have you ever felt hungry? Can you say when? Has someone you know ever been late? How did you feel as you waited for them? Did your feelings change when they finally appeared?* Always be prepared to follow the children's comments, interests and ideas, for example, when they talk about how they would react in similar situations. Draw attention to and emphasise the importance of illustrations in enhancing the story, for example, to portray the moods of the Great Storm-Cat.

Finally, encourage the children to recall these discussions when they share their initial opinions about the book. Emphasise that not everyone will have the same responses, and that some people will like particular aspects while others will dislike them. Comment, too, that opinions can change with subsequent readings.

Subsequent readings

After sharing the enjoyment of a first reading, plan further readings to extend children's comprehension of the text, develop their fluency in reading aloud and support their understanding of sentence structure, punctuation and spelling. The children should be taught to:
● use a range of decoding strategies for unfamiliar

Guided reading

words, check for meaning and self-correct errors
- build up words and understand spelling patterns in context
- read high frequency words on sight
- develop understanding of sentence construction and punctuation
- read aloud with pace and expression appropriate to the grammar of the text
- track the text from left to right and word by word
- understand and use book- and print-related terms correctly
- identify story elements (plot, character, setting)
- predict and infer
- sequence story events.

Setting the scene

Invite the children to read the opening page of the story together. Ask: *What does this tell us about where the story is set? Why is the harbour called 'the Mousehole'? Has anyone ever visited or stayed at a fishing village like Mousehole (or even at Mousehole itself)? What do you remember about it? Does this opening page tell us about any of the characters in the story? Can you name them? What do we find out about them?* Talk about the illustration on the facing page and ask if this adds further information to the facts about Mousehole, Tom and Mowzer.

Moving along

Read the story together and draw attention to words that connect ideas from one paragraph to another to help the flow of the story, for example, *And, So, But, Then, Soon, As, And again*. Read the last page while the children listen, this time missing out *And every year* at the start of each paragraph so that the text sounds more disjointed. Suggest thinking of different or more complex connective words to replace some of the connecting words on the page, for example, 'After that', 'Before long', 'Eventually', 'Meanwhile' and 'Finally'.

Evidence of change

Explain that stories often help us to learn more about the time in which they were set and that this book is about life in Victorian times, more than 100 years ago. Invite the children to focus carefully on the detailed book illustrations and make comparisons with how things look today. Explore the clothes of the women and children, and single items such as the lantern or candlestick. Find text evidence in phrases such as *set candles in all their windows* and *soused scad*.

Mowzer's family

The description of Mowzer's family near the beginning of the story tells us a great deal in two pages. Just as Mowzer has Tom for a pet, her children have people to help them. We know that her eldest son kept the quayside inn and one of her daughters kept the corner shop. Ask the children to describe the inn and the shop from the words they read. Ask: *What do you know about the inn? Why did Mowzer stay away from it? What sort of occupations do you think Mowzer's other kittens had? Do you think the people of Mousehole will have the same occupations today as they did in Victorian times? How might they have changed?*

Real or imaginary?

Explain that *The Mousehole Cat* was inspired by the legend of Tom Bawcock. Discuss how a real event can become a legend as it is passed from one generation to another, with storytellers adding their own ideas about what happened and removing those that they might not wish to include. The author of *The Mousehole Cat* has retold this legend in her own way. Ask: *How much of the story do you think could be true? Do you think that there was a storm, that Tom was a real person and the Great Storm-Cat and Mowzer were real cats?*

Explore the book illustrations together to find things that led Mowzer to interpret the storm as an angry cat, for example, the representation of the curling wave entering the gap in the harbour

Guided reading

wall as a huge cat's paw with sharp claws. Now read the author's words describing the same scene: *The sea drew itself up into giant waves and flung itself against the great breakwaters… But it could not get into the Mousehole.* When the author explains it through Mowzer's eyes, it becomes: *the Great Storm-Cat clawed with his giant cat's paw through the gap in the harbour wall.* Ask the children which version they prefer.

Book review

After discussing the story, the characters in detail, invite the children to reconsider their original impressions of the book through personal responses. Extend your original questions and give positive encouragement to help them to voice their opinions with confidence and clarity. Ask: *Have your opinions about the story changed since our first discussion? What is different? Would you change the illustration on the book cover now that you have read the whole story? What was your favourite part of the story? Was there any part of the story that you did not enjoy? Who do you think the main character is? Is there anything that you particularly liked or disliked about this character? Did your feelings towards the Great Storm-Cat change at different points in the story? How important are the illustrations to this story? How do you feel about the story ending?*

Shared reading

Extract 1

● Display an enlarged copy of the extract and cover the adjectives, *blue-green, high, tiny, fishing* and *winter* in the first paragraph. Encourage the children to read the text together, pausing to think of suitable words to replace those that are missing. Ask questions to help them, for example: *What colour might the sea be? What type of boats might be in the harbours?*

● Discuss the purpose of the extract. Ask: *What do these opening paragraphs tell us? Can we say who the main characters is? Do we know where the story is set? Can you find the words that are frequently used as opening words for a story? (Once there lived…). What is unusual about their position?* (They are not part of the opening sentence.)

● Ask the children to circle the capital letter at the start of each sentence and the full stop at the end. Ask: *Can you find the capital letters at the beginning of the names of people and places? Why are the words* the Mousehole *and* Mowzel *in speech marks?*

Extract 2

● Read an enlarged copy of the extract together. Invite the children to identify the days of the week and take turns to underline them. Ask: *Do you enjoy reading a page that follows a sequence so that you can predict what is coming next?*

● Identify the meal for Monday and ask the children if they can tell from the text what *morgy-broth* is (fish stew). Make a list of the words that describe cooking methods, for example, *baked, grilled* and *fried*. Ask the children what they think *ling, fairmaids, launces* and *scad* are in the context of the extract (types of fish or fish dishes; *fairmaids* are salted pilchards), and explain the meaning of unusual words such as *soused* (pickled).

● Ask the children to find the letters 'ed' at the end of the words *baked, topped* and *cooked* and draw a circle around them. Read the words with and without these letters and discuss their purpose (past tense).

● Comment on the decorative border. Ask: *How does the artwork link with the content?*

Extract 3

● Display an enlarged copy of the extract and read it aloud together. Encourage the children to use their knowledge of high frequency words to recognise alternative ways of spelling graphemes already taught, such as *night, Mousehole* and *raise*. Explain the meaning of unusual words such as *peril, haven* and *quayside*.

● Discuss how the words are grouped into paragraphs, each providing separate pieces of information. Ask: *What do we discover from each paragraph? Which three words connect each paragraph and help the whole page to flow?* Work as a class to create another paragraph to fit on the page, for example: *And every year the lighthouses along the coast flash their lights to the memory of old Tom and Mowzer.*

● Explore the artwork on the page and discuss how this extends the text information (the main image tells us that the curious Mousehole cats gather in the light of the open door to watch the villagers as they celebrate every year). Ask the children to comment on how well the decorative borders reflect the setting for the story ending.

Extract 1

At the far end of England, a land of rocks and moorland stretches itself into a blue-green sea. Between its high headlands lie tiny sheltering harbours where the fishing boats hide when the winter storms are blowing.

One of these harbours is so small and the entrance between its great stone breakwaters is so narrow that fishermen called it "the Mousehole".

The people who lived in the cottages around the harbour grew fond of the name and they call their village Mousehole to this day. They say it in the Cornish way, "Mowzel", but you may say it as you choose.

Text © 1990 Antonia Barber; Illustrations © 1990 Nicola Bayley.

Extract 2

So, on Mondays they made morgy-broth,
Mowzer's favourite fish stew.
On Tuesdays they baked hake and
topped it with golden mashed potatoes.
On Wednesdays they cooked kedgeree
with delicious smoked ling.
On Thursdays they grilled fairmaids,
a mouth-watering meal.
On Fridays they fried launces with a
knob of butter and a squeeze of lemon.
On Saturdays they soused scad with
vinegar and onions.
And on Sundays they made star-gazy pie
with prime pilchards in pastry.

Text © 1990 Antonia Barber; Illustrations © 1990 Nicola Bayley.

Extract 3

And every year since that day, at the inn on the quayside, the people of Mousehole hold a fish-feast on the night before Christmas Eve and raise their glasses to the memory of old Tom.

And every year, in the yard at the back of the inn, the cats of Mousehole gather and raise a great howling to the memory of old Mowzer.

And every year, folk come from all over Cornwall at Christmas time, to see Mousehole lit up with a thousand lights, shining their message of hope and a safe haven to all those who pass in peril of the sea.

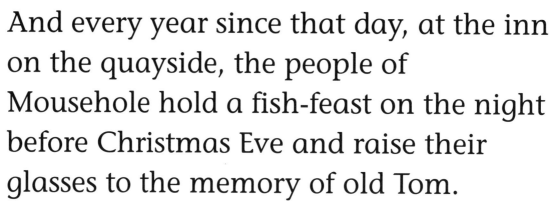

Plot, character and setting

Finding out about Mowzer

Objective: To explain their views to others in a small group, decide how to report the group's views to the class.
What you need: Copies of *The Mousehole Cat*, an enlarged copy of photocopiable page 15 and a copy for each group.
Cross-curricular link: PSHE.

What to do
● Read the story to the class and ask the children to find evidence of the character of Mowzer in the text and illustrations.
● Display an enlarged copy of photocopiable page 15. Read the words in the boxes together and decide which ones apply to Mowzer. Ask the children for additional word suggestions and write them on the board. Explain that these words will be useful when writing Mowzer's character profile.
● Divide the class into groups and give each group

a copy of photocopiable page 15 and extra paper for sentence drafts. Encourage the children to share individual ideas about Mowzer's character and appearance before coming to a group choice. Suggest that the groups nominate one person to write down their ideas and final character profile for Mowzer.
● Bring the class together and invite each group to choose a spokesperson to read their profile.
● As a class, decide which is the most appropriate character representation.

Differentiation
For older/more confident learners: Ask groups of children to complete character profiles for old Tom and the Great Storm-Cat.
For younger/less confident learners: Complete photocopiable page 15 with pairs of children, reading the words with them and asking appropriate questions, for example: *Do you think Mowzer is a brown cat?*

True or false?

Objective: To read more challenging texts which can be decoded using their acquired phonic knowledge and skills, along with automatic recognition of high frequency words.
What you need: Copies of *The Mousehole Cat*, an enlarged copy of photocopiable page 16 and a copy for each child, scissors.

What to do
● Explain to the children that you would like them to decide whether some simple statements are true or false, for example, *Today is Monday*.
● Invite individuals to make up some statements and say them aloud. Ask the other children to respond by saying 'true' or 'false'.
● Display an enlarged copy of photocopiable page 16 and explain that the statements are all about Mowzer. Read the first two sentences and decide whether they are true or false.

● Give the children individual copies of photocopiable page 16 and explain that they should cut out the statements and decide if each one is true or false, challenge the children to then make up some 'true' and 'false' statements of their own.
● Bring the class together so that individuals can read their statements while others decide whether they are true or false.

Differentiation
For older/more confident learners: Ask the children to write down true versions of the false sentences on the sheet.
For younger/less confident learners: Cut out and then read each statement from the page to the children and ask them questions about it, for example: *Did Mowzer really live in a shop? Did Mowzer love old Tom?* Arrange the strips in two piles to reflect their responses.

Plot, character and setting

A human pet

Objective: To identify the main events and characters in stories, and find specific information in simple texts.
What you need: Copies of *The Mousehole Cat*.
Cross-curricular link: PSHE.

What to do

● Read *The Mousehole Cat* and draw attention to the words on the first page saying that Mowzer had an old fisherman named Tom. This implies that Tom is Mowzer's pet rather than the other way around. Ask the children who they think was the real pet – Mowzer or Tom. Perhaps they think they both fulfil the role of a pet? Find similar references in the book that imply that the people are the pets, for example, *Mowzer felt that her children had not trained their people properly*.
● Invite the children to discuss with a partner the things that Mowzer and Tom did for one another and to imagine what it would be like to be an animal with a human pet. Ask them to decide what sort of animal they would like to be and the things they would do with their human pet.
● Bring the children together so that each pair can describe the animal they have chosen to be and the human pet they care for.

Differentiation
For older/more confident learners: Ask the children to pretend they are Mowzer and write about the relationship they have with old Tom.
For younger/less confident learners: Encourage the children to talk about their relationships with their own pets and make links to the relationship between Tom and Mowzer.

Now Mowzer, my handsome!

Objective: To explore familiar themes and characters through improvisation and role play.
What you need: Copies of *The Mousehole Cat*, men's dark blue pullovers and coloured neckerchiefs.
Cross-curricular links: Drama, PSHE.

What to do

● Read the page beginning *Then at last one evening*, when old Tom tells Mowzer that he must go fishing to save the people of the village. Through discussion, ensure that familiar phrases are fully understood, for example, *my handsome, stand by, come what may, without a catch*.
● Ask: *Why did Tom think he should go fishing instead of any of the other men in the village?* (They had families and he had none.) *What do Tom's words tell us about his character?* (He is courteous, caring and brave.) *How did Mowzer react to Tom's words? How did she communicate her feelings?* (She purred to tell him she understood/felt the same as he did; she purred loudly to say she would go as well/was worried about him.)
● Organise the class into threes so that they can improvise this scene, taking on the roles of the narrator, Tom and Mowzer.
● Bring the class together to share their improvisations and give constructive feedback to one another.

Differentiation
For older/more confident learners: Ask the children to choose other significant scenes from the story to re-enact, such as Tom and Mowzer's homecoming.
For younger/less confident learners: Set up Tom's kitchen in the role-play area, and include a soft toy cat, so that children can freely improvise the roles of Tom and Mowzer.

Plot, character and setting

The Great Storm-Cat

> **Objective:** To make adventurous word and language choices appropriate to the style and purpose of the text.
> **What you need:** Copies of *The Mousehole Cat*.

What to do

● Read the page describing the arrival of the storm, beginning *Then one year there came a terrible winter.* Draw attention to words describing how ferocious the storm was, for example, *the sea drew itself up into giant waves.*

● Ask the children if they can think of any exciting words to describe a storm and write them on the board. Introduce more adventurous examples of your own if necessary.

● Discuss how Mowzer sees the storm as an angry cat searching for mice hiding in a mousehole. Explore the accompanying illustration and ask the children to find the Great Storm-Cat's claws. Read out words describing Mowzer's viewpoint and invite the children to think of additional words reflecting this viewpoint. Write their suggestions on the board.

● Divide the class into an even number of groups. Ask half of the groups to discuss and then write a short description of the storm from Mowzer's viewpoint. Ask the other half to do the same from old Tom's viewpoint.

● Bring the class together to share their descriptions and make comparisons. Which viewpoints contain the most adventurous word and language choices?

> **Differentiation**
> **For older/more confident learners:** Invite the children to write about a storm from different viewpoints, such as a lighthouse keeper and a seal.
> **For younger/less confident learners:** Encourage the children to imagine they are out in a storm and ask them to talk about how they feel.

Beginning, middle and end

> **Objective:** To read independently and with increasing fluency longer and less familiar texts.
> **What you need:** Copies of *The Mousehole Cat*; an enlarged copy of photocopiable page 17 and a copy for each pair of children, scissors.

What to do

● Display an enlarged version of photocopiable page 17 on the board and read the sentences together as they appear on the sheet. Ask the children if the sentences tell the story in the correct order.

● Explain that this story is different because it has two beginnings. Establish that the first three paragraphs in the book explain where the story is set and how the village got its name, and the last two introduce the main character. Decide together which two sentences on the sheet should represent the beginning of the story.

● Discuss which sentences describe events from the middle and end of the story.

● Invite the children to work in pairs. Provide each pair with a copy of the photocopiable sheet and scissors to cut out the sentences and arrange them in their chosen order.

● Bring the class together to share their sequences. Are any in the same order? Which is the most accurate sequence?

> **Differentiation**
> **For older/more confident learners:** Invite the children to write beginning, middle and end sentences from a favourite story, cut them out and reassemble them in order.
> **For younger/less confident learners:** Create a simplified version of photocopiable page 17, with five short sentences from a well-known story.

Plot, character and setting

Holidaying in Mousehole

> **Objective:** To explain their reactions to texts, commenting on important aspects.
> **What you need:** Copies of *The Mousehole Cat*, a map of Great Britain, tourist guides about Cornwall, images of Mousehole.
> **Cross-curricular link:** Geography.

What to do

● Ask the children for their impressions of the village of Mousehole after listening to the story and exploring the text and illustrations in the book. Explain that, although it is a book of fiction, *The Mousehole Cat* is set in a real place in Cornwall called Mousehole and information about it can be found in many places in the book. Ask: *Is Mousehole in the country or by the sea? Who lives there? What are the buildings like?*

● Explain to the children that you are thinking of going for a holiday in Mousehole and you want to know more about where to stay, what to do and so on. Invite them to work in small groups to compile information about Mousehole from their knowledge of the story, book illustrations, web searches, leaflets and maps. Invite them to put together the most important aspects of the information they have gathered as a leaflet with pictures, maps and text.

● Set up a Mousehole display and discussion area with the children's work and the resources they used for their research.

> **Differentiation**
> **For older/more confident learners:** Invite the children to design a poster encouraging people to take a holiday in Mousehole.
> **For younger/less confident learners:** Look at the image of Mousehole on the inner title page and invite children to draw their own picture of it.

Calming the storm

> **Objective:** To listen to each other's views and preferences, agree the next steps to take and identify contributions by each group member.
> **What you need:** Copies of *The Mousehole Cat*, an enlarged copy of photocopiable page 18 and a copy for each pair of children.

What to do

● Read *The Mousehole Cat* and ask the children to think about Mowzer's feelings towards the wailing Great Storm-Cat. Ask: *Why does Mowzer feel sorry for the Great Storm-Cat? What does she do to calm him?*

● Display the enlarged version of photocopiable page 18 on the board and read the instructions. Work through the sentences in the boxes, asking the children how they think the Great Storm-Cat responded to Mowzer's actions each time. (Read the appropriate section in the book if they require further support.)

● Invite the children to work in pairs and supply each pair with a copy of photocopiable page 18 to complete. Suggest that they refer to the completed sentences as they decide how to dramatise the Great Storm-Cat's response to Mowzer's actions. Encourage the children to try to imagine what a cat 'singing like a siren' would sound like.

● Bring the class together to share their dramatisations and give supportive comments to one another.

> **Differentiation**
> **For older/more confident learners:** Ask the children to work in groups of four to dramatise a different section of the story.
> **For younger/less confident learners:** Help the children to complete the sentences, explaining the meaning of words and phrases, such as 'siren' and 'taken off guard'.

Plot, character and setting

Finding out about Mowzer

● Read the words below and underline the ones that describe Mowzer's appearance.

brown cat	**white paws**	**long whiskers**	**big dog**
golden eyes	**black and white fur**	**long floppy ears**	

● Now write some words of your own to describe Mowzer's appearance.

● Read the words below and underline the ones that describe Mowzer's character.

kind   wicked   brave   grumpy   contented   mean   loyal

● Now write some words of your own to describe Mowzer's character.

● Use some of the words you have underlined and your own words in sentences about Mowzer.

Plot, character and setting

True or false?

● Cut out the sentences, read them and then arrange them in two groups, 'True statements' and 'False statements'.

Mowzer had never had any kittens.
Mowzer had an old fisherman named Tom.
Mowzer did not like fish.
Mowzer stayed at home when Tom went out in the storm.
Mowzer loved old Tom very much.
Mowzer made the Great Storm-Cat feel calm again.
Mowzer liked to sit on old Tom's knee by a friendly fire.
Mowzer was a ginger cat.

● Now make up your own 'true' and 'false' sentences about Mowzer.

Plot, character and setting

Beginning, middle and end

● Cut out the sentences in the boxes and arrange them in the correct order to tell the story.

The next morning they set out very early, before the others were waking.
Mowzer watched as the Great Storm-Cat clawed with his giant cat's paw through the gap in the harbour wall.
Then one year there came a terrible winter.
Then, people and cats, they feasted together.
At the far end of England, a land of rocks and moorland stretches itself out into a blue-green sea.
Then the Great Storm-Cat played with them as a cat plays with a mouse.
And every year, folk come from all over Cornwall at Christmas time.
Once there lived in the village a cat whose name was Mowzer.
Then the Great Storm-Cat began to purr with Mowzer.

Plot, character and setting

Calming the storm

● Cut out the boxes below and arrange them in pairs to make sentences showing how the Great Storm-Cat responded to Mowzer's actions.

● Use your completed sentences to act out this part of the story with a partner.

When Mowzer sang like a siren…	the Great Storm-Cat played with them as a cat plays with a mouse.
When the little boat passed through the Mousehole…	the Great Storm-Cat grew quiet and began to purr with Mowzer.
When Mowzer sang again, longer and louder…	the Great Storm-Cat was taken off guard and the little boat left the harbour.
When Mowzer began to purr…	the Great Storm-Cat paused in his play and sang with her.

Talk about it

In the hot-seat

Objective: To ask and answer questions, make relevant contributions, offer suggestions and take turns.
What you need: Copies of *The Mousehole Cat*; an enlarged copy of photocopiable page 22 and a copy for each group.
Cross-curricular link: PSHE.

What to do

● Read *The Mousehole Cat* and discuss the effects of the storm on the village. Can the children imagine what it is like to be hungry?
● Show the children the character cards on photocopiable page 22. Read the descriptions and explain that they are all people who live in Mousehole. Discuss the different ways these people might be affected by the storm.
● As a class, discuss questions that the children would like to ask the characters, for example: *How did you feel when the big storm began? What*

worried you most during the big storm? What did it feel like to be very hungry? How did you feel when you were waiting on the harbour wall for Tom and Mowzer to return safely? How will you celebrate the end of the big storm?
● Put the children into small groups and give each group photocopiable page 22. Invite each child to pick a character card and take turns to be in the 'hot-seat' while others ask questions.
● Bring the class together to discuss their differing responses to the questions and invite volunteers to be in the hot-seat.

Differentiation
For older/more confident learners: Encourage pairs of children to invent a question/answer dialogue between two villagers.
For younger/less confident learners: Ask simple questions relevant to the children's personal experiences, for example: *What do you do when you feel hungry?*

Passing down a legend

Objective: To retell stories, ordering events using story language.
What you need: Copies of *The Mousehole Cat*, writing materials.

What to do

● Read the dedication by the author inside *The Mousehole Cat*. Draw attention to the words *This story was inspired by the old Cornish legend of Tom Bawcock*. Discuss the meaning of 'legend' and explain how legends used to be passed from one generation to another as stories told to children by older family members. Tom Bawcock was probably a very brave fisherman who did indeed set sail during a storm to net fish for the villagers, and the author's story is one version of this legend.
● Put the children into groups and ask each group to pretend they are family members

passing on the legend of Tom to younger relatives. Suggest that they divide the story into sections and tell one section each, for example, 'Introducing Mowzer and Tom', 'The arrival of the Great Storm-Cat', 'The taming of the Great Storm-Cat' and 'Bringing home the catch'.
● Provide each group with writing materials to make notes to ensure that events from the story are told in the correct order.
● Bring the class together to share their legends. Encourage constructive comments about the content and language used.

Differentiation
For older/more confident learners: Ask the children to pretend to be storytellers, passing on anecdotes about family events.
For younger/less confident learners: Ask the children to retell a repetitive familiar story in the correct order, such as 'The Enormous Turnip'.

Talk about it

What's in a name?

> **Objective:** To take turns to speak, listen to each other's suggestions and talk about what they are going to do.
> **What you need:** Copies of *The Mousehole Cat*, photocopiable page 23, atlases, maps.
> **Cross-curricular link:** Geography.

What to do
● Discuss how the name 'Mousehole' might have originated by looking at the Mousehole image on the inner title page and asking the children to find the 'mouse hole' in the harbour wall.
● Divide the children into groups and give them a copy of photocopiable page 23. Can they find Mousehole on the map? Can they guess why the surrounding area is prone to fierce storms? (It is exposed to the Atlantic.) Why was Mousehole protected in the story? (Because the harbour walls kept the storm at bay.)

● Ask the children to speculate on the origins of the other places on the map. Encourage them to attempt to read and spell unfamiliar words and highlight the most interesting ones. They could also search through atlases and maps for interesting place names that they might use in a story and add these to the map.
● Come together to share ideas and speculate on the origins of some of the names.
● Invite the children to use the most interesting names in individual short stories.

> **Differentiation**
> **For older/more confident learners:** Extend the activity by asking the children to invent place names for stories that they know, such as 'Treetop Towers' and 'Dinosaur Hill'.
> **For younger/less confident learners:** Find phonically regular names for the children to read, for example, 'Blackpool'.

Can you help me?

> **Objective:** To give some reasons why things happen or characters change.
> **What you need:** Copies of *The Mousehole Cat*, an enlarged copy of photocopiable page 24 and a copy for each pair of children.
> **Cross-curricular link:** PSHE.

What to do
● Read *The Mousehole Cat* and talk through the reasons why events, such as the big storm, created problems for the characters. Ask: *Have you ever had a problem? What caused it? How did it make you feel? How did you solve it? Did you ask for help?*
● Read the page starting *Then at last one evening*. Focus on Tom's problem about how to prevent the village children from starving. Do the children agree with his decision to go fishing? What else could he have done?
● Tom's problem created a problem for Mowzer

too. Ask the children why they think she decided to go fishing with him, and whether they would have done the same.
● Display an enlarged copy of photocopiable page 24. Read Tom's problem and discuss what led to it. Discuss ways of solving it. Do the same with the remaining problems.
● Ask the children to work in pairs and give each child a copy of the photocopiable sheet. Invite them to discuss their ideas then jot down their responses on the sheet.
● Bring the class together to discuss similarities and differences in their responses.

> **Differentiation**
> **For older/more confident learners:** Invite the children to invent problems and ask their partners for help in solving them.
> **For younger/less confident learners:** Support the children by talking through suitable options to help them with their responses.

Talk about it

Character conversations

> **Objective:** To explore familiar themes and characters through improvisation and role-play.
> **What you need:** Copies of *The Mousehole Cat*.
> **Cross-curricular link:** Drama.

What to do

● Read *The Mousehole Cat*. Focus on the words from *Many a tom-cat had Mowzer tamed in her time* to the end of the next page. Talk about how Mowzer decided to tame the Great Storm-Cat with her singing and how he reacted.
● Make comparisons between Mowzer and the Great Storm-Cat, the two cats in the story. Ask: *Are the two characters similar in any way? What is the main difference between them?*
● Ask the children to work in pairs so that they can explore the cat characters through role play. Ask them to begin by deciding which character role each child will take.

● Recall the page you have just read as a class and suggest that each pair makes up the possible conversation the two cats might have had during this first meeting. Suggest that they try a few different options.
● Bring the class together to re-enact their conversations. Invite the children to share constructive comments about the way that each pair has represented the two characters.

> **Differentiation**
> **For older/more confident learners:** Encourage pairs of children to explore other possible encounters between main characters and those who are lesser known, for example, Tom and a younger fisherman.
> **For younger/less confident learners:** Take on the role of one of the cats and ask questions to encourage appropriate responses, for example: *Why are you so sad and lonely? Shall I sing you a song?*

The long wait

> **Objective:** To consider how mood and atmosphere are created in live or recorded performance.
> **What you need:** Copies of *The Mousehole Cat*, children's outdoor clothing, toy or paper lanterns.
> **Cross-curricular link:** Drama.

What to do

● Read the page towards the end of *The Mousehole Cat* that starts with the words *Night fell*, and explore the illustrations together. Discuss how the Mousehole inhabitants might have felt as they waited for Tom and Mowzer to return. Ask: *How did the people know that Tom and Mowzer were still at sea? What did they do to guide them home again? What would their mood be as they waited?* Provide suitable words to help them to describe this mood, for example, 'anxious', 'worried', 'concerned'.
● Read on and discuss how the mood and atmosphere changed when the people knew their friends were safe. Ask: *How do you think the villagers felt when they spied the small boat returning?*
● Divide the class into groups and provide them with toy or paper lanterns. Ask each child to dress in outdoor clothing to take on the role of villager. Encourage them to discuss what they might say and how they might behave as they wait on the harbour wall.
● Allow time for each group to develop a short dramatisation of the harbour scene before asking them to perform to one another. Encourage questions and constructive comments after each performance.

> **Differentiation**
> **For older/more confident learners:** Invite children to write a short script depicting the same event.
> **For younger/less confident learners:** Join the children in role to model emotive vocabulary and appropriate body language.

READ & RESPOND: Activities based on The Mousehole Cat

Talk about it

In the hot-seat

● Choose one of the characters and talk about how they might feel about the events in Mousehole. Take turns to take the hot-seat and answer questions from your group in role as your character.

An old fisherman

A mother with a large family

A teenage boy learning to be a fisherman

One of Mowzer's kittens

A young girl

An old woman who has always lived in Mousehole

Talk about it

What's in a name?

● Read the place names and, as a group, talk about how the places may have got these names. Think about and share some of the stories and events that could have taken place there.

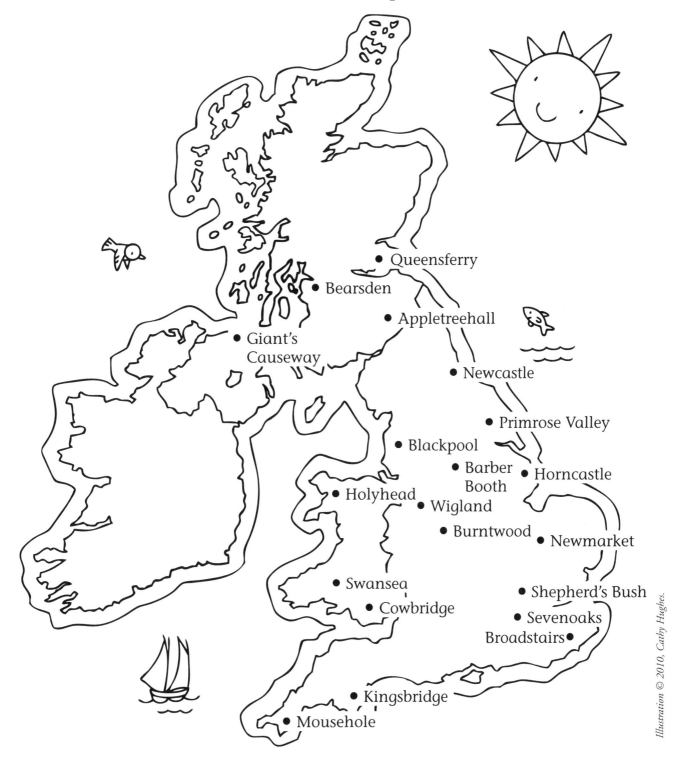

Queensferry

Bearsden

Appletreehall

Giant's
Causeway

Newcastle

Primrose Valley

Blackpool

Barber
Booth

Horncastle

Holyhead

Wigland

Burntwood

Newmarket

Swansea

Shepherd's Bush

Cowbridge

Sevenoaks

Broadstairs

Kingsbridge

Mousehole

Illustration © 2010, Cathy Hughes.

Talk about it

Can you help me?

● Some of the characters in the story have come to you for help with their problems. Discuss your ideas with a partner then write your responses in the spaces.

Tom

All of the village people are hungry because of the storm.
How can I help them?

Mowzer

Tom is thinking of going out in the storm by himself.
I want to stay by the warm fire. Why should I go with him?

The Great Storm-Cat

I am very angry hunting for men-mice in the stormy mousehole.
What will make me feel calm again?

A fisherman from the village

Tom's boat is missing and he is out in this terrible storm.
How can I help him to find his way home again?

PHOTOCOPIABLE

PAGE
24

www.scholastic.co.uk

READ & RESPOND: Activities based on The Mousehole Cat

Get writing

Past and present

> **Objective:** To convey information and ideas in simple non-narrative forms.
> **What you need:** A copy of *The Mousehole Cat* for each group.
> **Cross-curricular link:** History.

What to do

● Invite the children to look closely at images of single objects in *The Mousehole Cat*, such as the star-gazy pie, boot and candlestick. Ask questions to encourage them to compare the objects with modern-day equivalents, for example: *Do you use a candle in a candlestick to light a room? Have you ever eaten fish pie? Did your pie have fish heads peeping through the pastry? What do your boots look like?* Discuss the purpose of a kitchen range and compare this to modern ovens and fires.

● Divide the children into small groups and ask each group to look for evidence in the book of an aspect of life in Victorian Mousehole, for example, 'clothing', 'buildings' or 'kitchens'. Ask each group to make notes of their findings before writing out complete sentences to feed back to the class.

● Bring the class together to read their sentences and begin a comparison of life in Victorian Mousehole with life today.

● Ask the children to write a few sentences individually comparing life today with life in Mousehole in Victorian times. Compile the children's sentences into a class book.

> **Differentiation**
> **For older/more confident learners:** Invite the children to write a page from the diary of a Victorian child living in Mousehole.
> **For younger/less confident learners:** Ask the children to look at one of the children in the book, talk about the clothes they are wearing and compare these directly with their own clothes.

An imaginary sea creature

> **Objective:** To make adventurous word and language choices appropriate to the style and purpose of the text.
> **What you need:** Copies of *The Mousehole Cat*, an enlarged copy of photocopiable page 28 and a copy for each child.

What to do

● Discuss with the children whether the Great Storm-Cat was real or just in Mowzer's imagination. Perhaps the sight and sounds of the storm reminded her of an angry cat?

● Read the paragraph beginning *The Great Storm-Cat is stirring, thought Mowzer* and invite the children to imagine that they are Mowzer, looking through the cottage window and listening to the wind as it *whined like a wild thing about the high headlands.*

● Ask them to imagine that they can see and hear a strange and fantastic unknown creature out at sea. Discuss how this creature might look and smell, and the sounds it might make.

● Display the enlarged copy of photocopiable page 28 and read the questions together. Check that all the children understand what to do.

● Provide each child with the photocopiable sheet to complete. Encourage them to be adventurous with their imaginary creature and the language they use to describe it.

● Ask the children to write a short story with their imaginary creature as the main character.

> **Differentiation**
> **For older/more confident learners:** Invite the children to type and format their story in an appropriate style and font.
> **For younger/less confident learners:** Invite the children to draw a picture of their imaginary creature and help them to write a suitable caption underneath.

Get writing

Mouthwatering menus

> **Objective:** To create short simple texts on paper and on screen that combine words with images (and sounds).
> **What you need:** Copies of *The Mousehole Cat*, Extract 2 (from page 9), an enlarged copy of photocopiable page 29 and a copy for each child, writing and drawing materials, card, food magazines, glue sticks.

What to do

● Read Extract 2 on page 9 and discuss Mowzer's weekly menu. Ask: *Can you find the seven names of the fish dishes that Mowzer eats from Monday to Sunday?*

● Explain that fish was Mowzer's favourite food and that was why she ate it every day. Ask the children what they would choose for a favourite meal. Would they like to eat it every day? Ask them to invent the best weekly menu they can think of to include their favourite meals.

● Display the enlarged copy of photocopiable page 29 and read the instructions. Provide each child with a copy to complete along with materials to support their illustrations.

● Bring the class together to share their menus and comment on their meal choices.

● Provide groups with a large sheet of card, glue sticks, food magazines and scissors. Invite them to create a food collage. Ask them to stick their menus on the collage.

● Display the collages for the children to read and comment on.

> **Differentiation**
> **For older/more confident learners:** Invite children to write weekly plans with a specific focus, such as daily events.
> **For younger/less confident learners:** Support children with appropriate vocabulary to describe their favourite meals.

Tom's book of fish recipes

> **Objective:** To wordprocess short narrative and non-narrative texts.
> **What you need:** Copies of *The Mousehole Cat*, a copy of Extract 2 (page 9) for each child, cookery books, websites that include fish recipes.
> **Cross-curricular link:** ICT.

What to do

● Provide each child with a copy of Extract 2 on page 9 and look at the illustration in the book that links with this page. Identify the different fish that Tom uses in his recipes in the text and ask the children to underline them on their copies. Find words to describe the dishes Tom makes, such as *broth, stew, kedgeree* and *pie* and ask the children to circle these words.

● Discuss where Tom gets these recipes from. Perhaps he invents them, they may have been passed down from older members of his family, or maybe he has a fish recipe book.

● Invite the children to invent some new fish dishes for Tom and Mowzer. Talk about the usual components of a recipe, such as the name of the dish, the ingredients and step-by-step instructions. Make up an example on the board using the children's ideas.

● Divide the class into groups and ask each group to invent a fish recipe using cookery books and websites for ideas. After they have made notes they should type and print their recipe.

● Bring the groups together to share their recipes. Invite some children to compile them into a recipe book.

> **Differentiation**
> **For older/more confident learners:** Encourage the children to find images of fish on the internet to insert on their typed sheet.
> **For younger/less confident learners:** Explore a children's cookery book for a recipe idea.

Get writing

What if?

> **Objective:** To find and use new and interesting words and phrases, including story language.
> **What you need:** Copies of *The Mousehole Cat*, writing materials.

What to do

● Read *The Mousehole Cat* and draw attention to the happy ending on one page followed by the extension to the ending on the last page telling us that a feast is held every year in Mousehole in memory of old Tom. Ask: *Do you think the first ending about the village feast is a good one? Does the extra information on the last page make it more satisfying?*

● Explain that you would like the children to pretend that they have written *The Mousehole Cat* and that they are trying out different endings for it. Perhaps the Great Storm-Cat might decide to come home and live with Tom and Mowzer?

● Provide writing materials so that the children can make notes and draft their alternatives. Stress that they can be as adventurous as they wish with their ideas. Remind them about including story language.

● Bring the class together to share their endings and decide together which one is the most effective. Read the chosen ending in context, instead of the last two pages of the book.

> **Differentiation**
> **For older/more confident learners:** Suggest that the children invent an alternative ending to a favourite story.
> **For younger/less confident learners:** Familiarise the children with typical story language by asking them to join in with predictable endings such as 'happily ever after'.

Book review

> **Objective:** To maintain consistency in non-narrative, including purpose and tense.
> **What you need:** Copies of *The Mousehole Cat*, examples of book reviews, an enlarged copy of photocopiable page 30 and a copy for each child.

What to do

● Read *The Mousehole Cat* and invite the children to give their overall impressions of the book. Ask: *Did you enjoy this book? Was there anything you did not like about it? Did you feel that the illustrations added to the atmosphere of the book?*

● Explain the purpose of a book review and read the review on the back cover of the book, plus any other examples of reviews that you have.

● Invite the children to write their own review of *The Mousehole Cat* using photocopiable page 30. Display the photocopiable sheet and read through it a section at a time. Begin by discussing whether Victorian Mousehole is a good setting for a story. Continue, discussing the merits or possible shortcomings of characters, events and illustrations. Finally, consider a star rating out of five for the book.

● Provide the children with individual copies of the photocopiable sheet to use as a plan, prior to writing a book review based on the discussion and their follow-up notes.

> **Differentiation**
> **For older/more confident learners:** Invite the children to choose a different story to review, using the same approach.
> **For younger/less confident learners:** Focus on a favourite event in the book, for example, when Mowzer tamed the Great Storm-Cat. Ask them to draw a picture and write a suitable caption.

Get writing

An imaginary sea creature

- Draw a picture of your imaginary sea creature in the large box.
- Answer the questions in the small boxes underneath to describe your creature.

My imaginary sea creature

What is your creature called?	What does your creature look like?

What is the most unusual thing about your creature?	Where does your creature live?

What does your creature eat?	Does your creature have any friends?

Get writing

Mouthwatering menus

● Use the boxes to write down the name of your chosen meal for each day and to draw a picture of it.

The day	The dish of the day	What it looks like
Monday		
Tuesday		
Wednesday		
Thursday		
Friday		
Saturday		
Sunday		

READ & RESPOND: Activities based on The Mousehole Cat

Book review

● Use this sheet to help you to plan and write a book review for *The Mousehole Cat*. Finish the sentences in the boxes giving your opinions.

I think Mousehole is a good setting for a story because...

_____

I think that setting the story in the past makes it...

_____

I like the character of Mowzer because...

_____

I think the Great Storm-Cat is...

_____

My favourite story event is...

_____

A story event I would change is...

_____

I think the illustrations are important in this book because...

_____

Give the story a rating out of five by shading the stars.

Assessment

Assessment advice

Ongoing formative assessments of individual achievements and progress in literacy are an essential component of the planning and assessment cycle. They help teachers to make valuable judgements about a child's progress and provide supportive evidence when ensuring that future learning activities are planned at an appropriate level. Assessment outcomes are invaluable in determining new individual targets. Reports and assessments should be based on clear evidence arising from observations and examples of work completed.

Formative assessments build up gradually and should be created from a variety of sources, such as observations, contributions to classroom discussions, peer group interaction and analysis of children's practical work. The importance of peer- and self-assessment should not be underestimated. The activities in this book are designed to be assessed using a combination of these methods.

Each activity in the book has a clear assessable learning objective that represents what a child should know, or be able to do, by the end of that activity. Informing children of these objectives before an activity begins is essential in order to help them to recognise their involvement in their own learning. At the end of each activity there should be time for reflection, when children can revisit the learning objective and discuss whether or not they think they have achieved it. This helps them to recognise the relevance of assessment in planning the next steps in learning.

You can use the assessment activity on photocopiable page 32 as part of a record of individual progress. It is also a useful tool for assessing a child's ability to plan and write a story on a given theme.

Real meets imaginary

> **Assessment focus:** To use planning to establish clear sections for writing.
> **What you need:** Copies of *The Mousehole Cat*, an enlarged copy of photocopiable page 32 and a copy for each child.

What to do

● Read *The Mousehole Cat* and discuss the encounter between Mowzer and the Great Storm-Cat. Talk about how Mowzer managed to tame the Great Storm-Cat so that she and Tom could continue fishing successfully.

● Recall previous discussions about imaginary sea creatures and explain that you would like the children to write a story about a real cat meeting an unusual imaginary creature, just as Mowzer did. They can be friends or enemies. Invite the children to share their initial ideas.

● Display the enlarged copy of photocopiable page 32 and read through it together. Using one of the children's ideas as an example, fill in the boxes together.

● Provide each child with a copy of the photocopiable sheet to plan their story. As the children are planning, interact with individuals to support their ideas. Encourage them to focus on the story structure with appropriate opening and closing words and a brief description of the main encounter. Promote inventiveness in their character descriptions and interactions.

● Invite the children to write out their stories in full, referring to their written plans.

● Bring the class together to comment constructively on the finished stories.

Real meets imaginary

● Use this sheet to plan and write your own story about what happens when a real cat and an unusual imaginary creature meet.

Title: _____

Main character: _____

Setting: _____

Who is the imaginary creature in the story? What is unusual about this creature?

Beginning
Make a note of words you are going to use to begin your story.

Middle
Make a note of the main event in the story.

End
Make a note of words you could use to end your story.